STRAYING TOWARD HOME

Also by James Mersmann

The Isis Poems
Allen Ginsberg
Out of the Vietnam Vortex

STRAYING TOWARD HOME

POEMS BY

James Mersmann

NewSouth Books
Montgomery | Louisville

NewSouth Books
P.O. Box 1588
Montgomery, AL 36102

Library of Congress Cataloging-in-Publication Data
Mersmann, James F., 1938-
Straying toward home / James Mersmann.
p. cm.
I. Title.
PS3613.E777S77 2003
811'.54--dc21
2003011014

ISBN-13: 978-1-60306-028-8
ISBN-10: 1-60306-028-6

Design by Randall Williams
Printed in the United States of America

Dedicated to
my father and mother
for solid ground
and a net
for tangling stars

CONTENTS

I.

LOSSES AND DEPARTURES

Dachau

I cannot say how the rain falling
on the stark gravel of Dachau
draws me back to childhood and my father's farm

except this field where Germans harvested hair
and granaries of bone is as square and large
as the far forty beyond the summer pasture

or that my brother who fought the Krauts
left us behind in the fields
to hoe and bring our harvests home.

We were farmboys who read books and saw
midsummer movies when the tent show
hit town. We took our heroes home, whinnying
like Trigger and peering over the pond bank
like a reconnoitering Alan Ladd. Our plowhorse
was Pegasus, and the bull bellowed
in his stall like the Minotaur.

Our brains were young, and all our work
was wild; every tool was a scimitar hungry
for the head of a Hun, a bazooka
ablaze in the face of a Jap.

Whether we pitched shit from the barn door
or revved the cornsheller's teeth
till they ripped cobs with a buzz saw roar,

all our labors were Herculean.

Before any of us found those wonderfully awaited
first heroic hairs at our crotch,
Dad put a hoe in our hands and pointed
to the bean fields, to acres of young corn

where a few weeds stood isolate and tall in the rows
like abandoned sentries, like snipers gone insane, exposed,
begging to be cut down by the perfect slash of John Wayne,
the bayonet of a battle-berserk Audie Murphy.

And here and there, where an enemy squad had survived
last year's war and scattered its seed
like dragons' teeth, there were whole armies
to kill, cocklebur hordes of Genghis Khan,
panzer platoons of sourdock.

We waded in hacking, till sweat rose
and our blades dripped green gore. We relished
the grunts that surprised our throats as we struck
again and again the heavy torsos of hempweed,
cut the feet from beneath the redroots, axed down
Goliath sunflowers that fell like redwoods. We cleared out

the bunkers of nested enemy and moved through,
and the going got easy again, only the occasional sniper
here and there standing between us
and the Paris of the water jug at the row's end.

In the next swath of the field we would encounter
scattered resistance in the area of the recent battle,

but it would be only a matter of mopping up—
and satisying in the sight of the strewn dead
already shrivelling in the noon heat.

It was a clean business we had there,
purifying our Aryan corn, and the soybeans,
leaving the long straight rows rolling perfect
under the stone eye of the summer sun.

Today at Dachau, a chill drizzle wavers in the wind
like a blown curtain; standing in the fenced field,
my arms hang down, without sinew.

Only the slow rain slashes
the squat rows of Jew-hut foundations,
and forty acres of small gravel drowns weedless and grey.

Oil for My Lamp

That day serenely alone in the woods
where I was both hermit and fugitive
as dusk fell and the shrouded light
in the ramshackle cabin grew too dim
to read one sentence more in Hawthorne's dark book,
I opened the rough cabinet beneath my bench,
and reached down, without looking,
for the kerosene can to stoke the lamp,
reached, as so many times before,
in habitual trust, dreamily,
my hand familiar with that space,
expecting light, and grasped
the snake's slick cold thickness,
held for a split-second, a chilling
handful of bone cold dark—
before we both moved quick.
He, somewhere unknown
into the cabin's bowel,
and I, into absolute upright
frozen clarity,
and the long, slow descrescendo
of breathing in the falling dark.

Divorce

In Kansas City, too, the stockyards
and shambles lie at the dark center—
from the black of the bull's eye
the city swirls buildings of white bone.

The slaughterpens of Wilson and Swift
and Armour Star steam
with a thousand bawling cattle,
and on each forehead swirls

a center of grace, a miraculous
god's eye of tufted hair,
a target,
and point of departure.

At great gray Cudahy
in stench thick as noise
the Hereford bull
shies into the knocker's chute

wide-eyed, flaring wet nostrils
at the terrible floor
and before his head can lift
—there! that rose-star of soft hair—

the mallet slams him splay-legged
a sudden black wall widens
loud in his skull

huging his eyes, stunning stiff time

to incredible slowness
his locked legs, rigid as a rocking horse,
quiver and hold, almost forever quiver and hold,
buckle and he falls
                    & falls

& falls slamming the final floor
a hook through the nose
skids the body forward

grapples the heels, jerking
the heavy butt rafterward
in a screel of pulleys,
the twisted neck, the nose smearing the concrete floor

then he feels a thin hot
gold thread drawn down
the seam of his belly
and watches the gut gutter
filling with his own entrails

until in the dimming cave that he is
a cold red wind begins to ache
and his upturned filming eye
draws tight with surprise
at such hunger.

After Visiting Pompeii

Some nights I stand, again,
stunned among the rich dead
streets and houses of Pompeii
in a trance of memory, staring
at the wine urns brimming
with ash, at the plaster casts—
of the dog just risen to bark;
of the man backed crouching into a corner
hands futilely upraised forever;
of the family fleeing the house stopped
midstride in a line in the yard—
and on the far horizon, the great mountain,
Vesuvius, serenely purple, sleeping in clouds.

Within easy shout of the mountain's mouth,
again I ride the train back to Naples
on glistening rails, past begrimed living
houses, wash on the line, brown-bellied babies
scooting from porches, grandmothers shaking
out aprons; at each stop loading and unloading
folks home to their suppers. I turn to a man
just hanging himself by his fists in the straps
and ask, in bad Italian, *how do you live here?*,
my eyes and head gesturing the mountain.

I am not ready for an answer so earnest,
so smouldering and full of molten words.

Non capisco, I say, *lentemente per favore.*
Non capisco! Parla lentemente!
But this rush of lava is beyond all damming;
he does not grab me by the collar
to tell me his tale—he needs his arms
to flail smoke from his words—
but his eyes are black and wild,
and I think, Coleridge was lucky
the ancient mariner wasn't Italian.

But what, then, I could not understand,
I have since translated, *or invented,* cinder
by cinder, in ashfall dreams where a hung man
gesticulates wildly in the spark and sputter
of a train in the suburbs of a volcano.

  Here, he says, here we know we are madmen
  living in the maw of a dragon, but you,
  what do you know of your madness?
  Your madness is to forget
  how fragile is the flame in your loins,
  how you waste your lives. You walk daily
  through the ricochet crossfires of rush hour,
  feeding a fat heart at the TV table;
  your midnight cigarette is a red eye glowing
  above the sour mattress of flammable loneliness.
  In hotel rooms you strip with strangers and dive
  into rocking tides of flesh, though death's
  thin finger picks everywhere now at the lock.
  And even if you live carefully and run long
  on the Sunday roads, church-coming Christians
  dressed in bowties and Buicks will run you down

because the streets must not belong to the flesh.
In your quick-marts, those tiny old ladies
with quivering mouths have pistols in their purses.
All your homes hover above the hollow guts
of coal mines, cling like gulls to the dandruff
sluff of cliffsides, huddle in the spume
of Chernobyl and Three-Mile Island; for years
mad presidents have sat hunched and smiling
over the buttons of doom. All of us live
on the 37th floor of the San Andreas fault.
And yet you believe somehow
you will live forever.

But here, watching the red sauce
oozing in steam over the heaped pasta
on our plates, our mortality, it is easy
to remember. Whatever pause it may give
quickens us, adds picante and salt
to our coiling forks; we touch
the children, reach for the wine—
in Chianti there is never a catastrophe.

Here we go on, we go on as we can, kissing
with grease on our mouth, loving
the sea and the light, knowing
each day is a grace, knowing the great lady
whose hills are vineyards and breasts,
may, like any wife, without warning, growl fire
from her throat, fling rocks at our heads.

How do we live here? We live
as everyone must who lives at all.

Wherever or however we live,
each of our hearts is a hand grenade
and all the pins are pulled.

The Not-So-Wild Swans at Windermere

At Coole Park, I had seen Yeats' nine
leftover swans asleep on the lake
in early morning, heads tucked
under their wings, each pair
separate and distant, keeping
their crystal territory
and ceremony of innocence.

But this evening at Lake Windermere,
swans come ashore to panhandle
tourists with passionate intensity.
Lacking all conviction, they duck and bow
for favors like an aging Wordsworth,
bullying mallards and pintails for crumbs.

Ah, you are a bunch of beauties, you are,
cruising in through the tied boats, sailing
your long loveliness in among the teal,
one webbed black foot out of the water, slung
over your back like a gangster hiding a gat.

And when you hiss and wobble ashore, you lose
your last grace, awkward as brides in black socks,
lamppost princesses in hookers' boots.

You would make Wagner throw down his music.
Swan-mad King Ludwig would become sane.
Thoreau was luckier chasing a loon.

Working all weathers, stony Jeffers loved
the Wild Swan ruffling her storm feathers
over the Pacific, and built his granite
tower in the blow of her wings.

Dreaming in a timber of myth, Yeats woke
in Gregory's woods when the wild rose
white and thundering: feather broke him
back to the purities of bone.

But at such harlots and hustlers, Leda
could only laugh. You are less like Zeus
than the stuffed parrot that lays plastic
eggs in the arcade box. Nor are you Juno
unless Juno bent over a bed for bucks.

And I myself sit like a tainted judge
on shit-stained docks, skimming the deep
waters, hacking another poet's terrain
while my home ground lies fallow in weeds.

Oh, how shall we recover our grace,
my fallen brothers and sisters?
How did we become so hungry for grease?
Who taught us the lace and thunder of wings
were evolved for the foraging of Fritos?
And how did we come to trail such fine feathers
among the shorewash of condoms and ice-cream sticks?

Assisi Night Thoughts

You lie down on the cold cobble of a black alley
to sleep like Francis in Francis's town. Above you
Sister Moon rises thin and chill in a scatter of stars.
One after another, lights in the houses go out.
The last walker outwalks his thoughts. On warmth
and ordinariness, the final door closes.

You do not know why you are here, alone,
shivering on the stones where Francis walked—
but long ago you learned the only way to find out
what you are doing is to do it, and pay attention.
We learn by going / where we have to go.

What you are tempted to think you are
doing is sacrificing for the poor. You see
yourself tomorrow, giving a street beggar
the hotel money, watch his double-take
when you drop 40,000 *lire* in his puffy hand.
(You do not yet know you are the beggar in Assisi.)
In another fantasy you see yourself after long hours
caught up in prayer, rapt like Francis
by a hand from a cloud. But you know so little
about prayer, and there are no clouds,

only icepick stars and stillness; and you
are frankly afraid, afraid of the strangeness
of what you are doing, afraid of the wind that rakes
the crooked streets, afraid of thieves and cutthroats

and Italian nightwatchmen, afraid of the icy constellations
Scorpio and Draco and all the unknown crawling possibilities
in a nighttime, foreign, and rocky place.

But the night and the cobble are a cold college
and you do learn. You learn how your childhood faith
has leaked through the sieve of stars, leaving them
empty and wonderfully sharp; how you would give back
such clarity for the warm lights of Assisi at dusk,
for the easy curl of incense and soft songs in the oratory
of St. Francis; how we would all almost gladly enter again
the smothering womb we fought our way out of, and why
so few ever leave it at all; how we miss the suckle
of certainties, how we long to crawl into the safe
lap of obedience, if only the ice of the stars
might gather and melt again in a soft red moon
that pulses like a heart behind full breasts
where we can push our head till our ears have vacuumed
to the smooth and delicious curve of warmth.

You learn how, light years from home, alone
on the cold streets of your knowing,
in your throat a hurt widens to suck
and murmur and glue yourself back
again to the warm sources. You learn
you know nothing at all about St. Francis.

Faith and knowledge speak different tongues,
but both speak beauty. Whether in the early glottals
and verbs of the blind and vowelled blood, or
the cold nouns and consonants of light, we who listen
have heard first one and then another unmistakable voice.

Trapped in one language, we struggle to speak the other.
But our longing is to be linguists of both languages,
to be touched at once by the perfect
finger of knowledge and the whole hot hand of love,
to hear and somehow say, all at once, the *Word/Flesh*;
to know that lone syllable that sings
as heat in stars, as light in stones:
that sound a saint can hear.

!What's that!?!
Is that you, Brother Francis,
moving in the shadows ? . . .

I lift up my beggar's hand.
Will you give me that single coin?
You who know this cold street,
you who know this thirst,
that whiskey sybillance.

Letting the Garden Go

Sluggish and fat in sweating midsummer,
I can only half remember how much hope
I sowed lush with the seeds
in early spring—the imagined vines
and fruit swollen heavy above the hoed loam.

And how the garden did for a time spring up
gay in its new leaf promise and blossom
with me at its center. Its loveliness,
its green symmetries and hubbub of bees
I loved more than any hoped-for harvest.

But could anyone, breaking the first brief rhubarb
from its hub before the heat burned the leaves back,
not have dreamed largesse of pies, rows
of preserves awaiting sweetened winter?
I did think, yes, there would be more
than just a few unbitten berries
stolen from under the gun
of the bluejay's bitching.

Now with a flat blade, August bats
all green back down, except the weeds that leap
up like scholars seeking national reputations,
strangling the light, breeding pustulas
and smutboils on the sweetcorn. Wilt and blight
blast cucurbit and bean, cankerworm and mold
promote themselves among the melons.

Gnawed tomatoes, chipmunk bitten,
bleed like Goya's wounded. The garden's heart
pivots in a mandala of pestilence.

It would be easy to turn and walk away,
choosing exile at the garden's edge. I could
write it off, leave it to the slugs,
let the kudzu extend her limitless insinuations,
inexorably greedy, all-swallowing and quick.

I don't want to ponder all the hacking
and flailing, all the poisons
and sacks of shit it will take
to bring the garden back.

No doubt every man's August was always like this.
Has anyone made it to autumn unstung by the blowfly
that flowers from the dead? Among the bitten leaves
I understand the ancient ultimatum—only by sweat
and bitter love will you make things grow.
Today I must take hold or let the garden go.

A Malhação de Judas

("The Whipping of Judas"—Brazilian folk ritual)

On Good Friday night, lightless
night of cold bone and black
blood in the imagination's tomb,
when Jesus and all that is generous
has stiffened to stone,

above the ancient towns of *Minas Gerais,*
the moon throws a black robe over her brow,
and in random house after house
man and wife, widow, and recluse, rise
in dark privacy, rigging the effigies
of whomever they hate most, neighbor
or politician, *sogra* or *dedo duro*—
any Judas that ever kissed them
and cried "Hail Rabbi!"

With wheat straw and wax, clothes and clay,
they shape private faces so outrageous
no one can mistake that nose, this brow;
and still to compose the riddling verse
to hang as accusation and insult, so

PORTUGUESE TERMS: *batedores*—beaters of drums or percussion instru-
ments; *bateria*—a band or group beating rhythm on whatever comes to
hand; *dedo duro*—"straight-" or "hard-finger," one who informed on or
pointed an accusatory finger at his neighbors during the military dictator-
ship; *malhação de judas*—the whipping of Judas; *malhadores*—those who
beat or whip; *Minas Gerais*—a province in the interior of Brazil; *sambistas*—
samba dancers; *sogra*—mother-in-law

both hated one and hater can be guessed . . .
but not proven.

And then when the sea eats at the shore
in the lightless last hour before dawn
you step out to hang your Judas
from someone's tree or gate, and in the crowding
dark wait for the first seep of light
in the lean streets, to walk
and see what elsewhere hate has hung,
and your own face, perhaps, in the neighbor's tree.

Then quick home before the light
can pare its black nails,
to the blind and shadowed
sash to wait the *malhadores*
who will come to thrash
your hanging wheat of hate.

When the sun comes
stropping a razor in the streets,
shirtless, shoeless boys in alleys wake,
and reach for sticks, remembering
at once and sharp, this
is the day, this is the day
love cries hate
and they may hit and hurt
for play. And one by one
they gather in a gang and come.

It is a lark at first, finding a Judas
here, then there, and giving him a whack—

a dance in the streets, a *samba*
that only slowly licks its chops.

And from the shuttered windows
people watch and smile

because the day is hot and the town
is full of Judases; and there is no ecstasy
like rhythming sweat and the beating
of *batedores* under the sun.

The crowd of boys grows larger and loud,
the frenzy swells,
and the stuffing flies.
And when the first hung man fails,
and from tree to ground
cracks down, the feet and sticks
of urchin *sambistas* kick and rage,
and the *samba* stings and slugs.

In the blinded houses
old muscles flex and rhyme.

When the boys grow weak—
and it takes a while!—
they fire the rags they struck
and watch the flames leap
and speak their smoking hate.

High on the hills
a herd of black goats
shifts uneasily

in the smell of fire.

In the darkened rooms, tongues
and eyes flicker and lick.

The boys recover breath and voice
and race to the next bastard hung
or nailed on high, and soon
the city freckles with fire;
this is the day that spite
and the sky can burn.

When the last Judas
and the sun come down,
the boys pitch to sleep
in their sweat; people
fall on beds and snore
after a night that has
lasted all day.

The light sheathes its last knife
and Holy Saturday dies in gray.

All the new night, smoke
lifts from the avenues
and wind picks the ashes away.

Next morning in the quiet streets
the sun comes walking in a light robe,
and all that rises is
rinsed and white.

Chilton County Woods:
Revisiting the Garden in Ruins

The fences have fallen,
the pine posts cut and skinned
in Alabama heat, rotted through in three years,
the wire still gleaming like new in the weeds.

I knew then they would not hold,
but the work was the need,
the perfect perfection of the line
of wire stretching into the trees
and the sweat rolling and purging the city
crud and a thousand years of bad marriage.

Alone I dug the holes, alone
sighted them in, and the poles
cut at a slant to shed the rain
stood straight, and my goats watched

as if wondering what it was I wanted
to wall away from them in this lost
nowhere of wilderness.

It was nothing but what is alive
because of human touch, whether radishes
or beans or truth, or something so simple
as your eyes watching now without lies

or something so old
as the arrowheads that sprouted in the lettuce rows

after rains, broken triangles of rose
quartz finely shaped and serrated
by a hand before Christ in a dream of animal thighs

or that single, tapered stone,
lifted by the thrusting asparagus,
chipped from chert and dropped by Clovis man, pointed
and waiting for me twelve thousand years,
that I, finding it, might at last
harvest one thing hard and whole.

II.

BREAKING
NEW GROUND

Western Variations on a Zen Aphorism

The finger is very useful for pointing at the moon,
but we must take care not to mistake it for the moon.

I.
The husk is very useful for protecting the seed,
but we must take care not to mistake it for the seed.

Nothing lives long in an unbroken shell:
whether chick or chickpea, it pecks at the husk
until the bright crust or pod splits away
and life leans out to say its name
in the syllables of things.

Public virtue hollow as a calabash
gleams loud like a drum.
But when a good man's
goodness blackens and cracks
in the public eye,
a weak white verb
at last mucks down
to utter silence
in the worm-quarried waste

and listens
in the Jonah dark to learn
to brace its pale toes
in flaking mica

and buckle its back
under the weight of virtue's
first, paired, nondescript leaves
and lift them out in garden light
like an offering,
like a child's hand,
like first words
whispering in a blather of weeds.

2.

The metaphor is very useful for expressing a truth,
but we must take care not to mistake it for a fact.

Look up from the book of metaphors,
from your sacred etymology of fear.
You must eat the apple of Eden, if you dine
from the orchard at all. There are no trees here
unblighted by the bite of sapience. Unless you
relinquish citizenship in the growing kingdom,
you must like all that lives twist and knuckle
in frost and fire along the painful spiral
toward the blister and heave of whatever is to be
your future fruit. And if you should ever really be

lucky enough to taste the whole nature
of evil, and still want it, Hell would be
no surprise, no outrageous wage.

Choose evil until you get it
by heart, and you will
want it no more.
Your choices will be over,

and you will have eyes.
The orchard blossoms
and light is windfall
forever, and bright.

Breaking New Ground

Everywhere, as if a cable from my elbow tows her,
my nine-year-old follows me like a small boat,
bobbing, spilling questions on all sides, shining.
Together we will begin the garden somewhere
in this new state, this strange yard
where I probe hardpan chert and clay
for a vulnerable spot, and one more try
in my transient's life for growing space.
She hears my spade bite like gritted teeth,
watches it bounce away empty. Already I am
counting the years I will need
to rebuild and restore life here.

"Is the soul any good, Dad?"
(Even before we came South, her tongue,
sometimes twisted, was never tied.)
"It's soil," I say. She tries
to taste the difference; turns it
on her tongue like a sweet mint.
"Soyerl," she says a dozen times
and can't shove the sound beyond
halfway. "That's okay, Sue," I say,
"at least I think you've found
the middle ground." She sees my smile
and knows there's something there
she hasn't got, but has her own
things to grow, and wanders off
tilling her syllables like rich loam.

"Soyerl, soryul," I hear her go—
and I know I, too,
have had some trouble
keeping the two
apart.

Lowering the Ceiling

"Them ceilings're too high," my neighbor says,
looking around the old house that's new to me.
"Can't heat all that wasted space you don't need

that much headroom you oughta lower'em that's what
I did it's cheap and easy come on
over across the street and see."

We go and find large squares of grainy tile
slung low on metal racks,
and no room to wear a Lincoln hat.

Both his furnace and his pride are up.
"Boy," he says, "now it's just as warm in here
as can be," and I agree, "It's mighty close."

His ceilings were nine-foot dropped to seven,
and he thinks mine, being eleven
should save me double, hung like his.

At the street we say goodbye and pivot
toward different lives and spaces.
At my door, I watch him disappear in his.

I envy him his cedars though, paired
at his porch, wedging green forty feet
into the blue. Except that years ago planted

too near the wall, they've shoved up
close and blacked his house's eyes.
Sucked into low darkness, he's warm.

In my house cold solstice light surfs
through high windows, exposing the ceiling's flaws.
The last owners hammered sheetrock

against ninety-year-old plaster, slapped mud
at the joints as if they were fools, or drunk;
but they left me headroom, all eleven feet

to stand up in, and for that I salute them
and devil-may-care recklessness, or whatever it was
that kept them at work over their heads.

I know old houses like this stay cool
in July when hummingbirds hover
in the trumpet trellis at the window,

and I like the way tall rooms teach
lovers the luxuries of cardigans
and rough afghans in woodsmoky winters.

The day may come when practicality demands
I lower my overhead, but not yet. I climb
a ladder, patch the few new cracks,

let the old, rough work stand as it is,
a trophy and tribute to something,
if to nothing more than abandon and clumsy size.

Stocking the Pond

The midnight pond dreams
in a lamination of moonlight.
On the clay banks, the coming
fescue lolls thinly
in an uncombed sheen, long
and limber as baby hair.

May be it is not moonglaze
but his own waiting
for the least sign
of fish to pimple the surface,
that seals the water
under this honey-thick skin of silence.

There may be fish beneath
the tongueless bloom of the moon's
mute unsplintered mirror,
but he did not see them go in.

Though he has seen fishmen
call their channel cats
to the surface to feed like hogs,
for three days nothing has risen
to the spatters of fishbread
cast on this blind eye.

His neighbor claims he watched
the hatchery man lug them

in buckets to the pond lip
in the bright dazzle of noon,
but he has to take the fish
as a matter of faith

and believe
somewhere in the depths
a slow cauldron of sulling catfish
are hugging the mud,
angry as headaches,
their long moiling whiskers
already foretelling the day
they will grow hungry enough
to stike at the floating moon.

To the moon the pond is
small and unlikely
as a bullet hole
in the mastodon's side, tinier
than a whale's eye,
the fish-dreaming man
a chigger at the edge
of an acne pock.
His past is a frayed shirttail,
his future an appointment
he'll remember a week too late.

Around him everywhere brightness is a lake,
but he aches with the whole dark
of all waiting

though inside him electrons boil
in shimmering orbits, and sulled fish
ready themselves to rise
in spangles of light.

Mockingbird

The mockingbird on the mailbox
is waiting for nothing. The sharp rings
of his eyes look out over the raised flag
past the neighbor's drive, down the empty road
where the mail jeep will importantly appear,
but what he sees is nothing. His head
is cocked back like a child thinking.
But he is not thinking. He is waiting
without waiting, for nothing. His feathers
lie quietly on his shoulders, shining.

In a moment he will also be waiting.
In a moment he may once for nothing shift
an inch along the Conestoga curve of the box.
He does not know when he will not be
waiting. He does not know when he will break
into flight or song. He is not waiting
to sing. His breast is empty. He is
not waiting for the hundred songs
that may in a moment pour into him
and out of him like water
from a burst hose, urgent and rainbowing.
He is not waiting for the space
that will reappear where he was
after the sudden white rowing, the semaphor
of his wings coding the light.

The Man in the Mirror Is Left-Handed

For more years than I want to name
I've lived in the same house with him, broken
his bread, shared lovers like Chang and Eng,
and never until this morning, noticed—
the man in the mirror is left-handed!

He was always difficult enough
when I cut his hair or trimmed his beard, but
still, he was as much like me as identical twins.
But now I see he does everything backwards:
parts his hair on the wrong side,
winks outrageously with his right eye,
reaches out for everything with that devil's hand.

Has he just started all this?
Or have I just begun to see? I wish
it were—but it's not—just optical.
If I go out right, he exits left.
And I thought I knew where I was going.

Now, how can I be sure he's not the one
who undoes all my good; if all night long
he unweaves my daylight tapestries
until his true mate—and sinister—arrives
to break out in open rebellion?
This noon in the dining room mirror
I caught him, the bastard, when I
moved my fork to the right, shifting his

just so to the left, countering all my moves.

There's probably no end to how far this goes.
I'm willing to bet he bats right
and throws left, and, sure, his car
has the steering wheel on the passenger side,
and he drives on the wrong side of the road
like the bloody British, and what's more,
this means he's been running all
the bases backwards, keeping the score down!

Oh, I've tried to improve the world!
But does it matter? Is the deuced score
always love and loveless level, perpetual
match point with the advantage
forever shifting back and forth across the net,
and no provisions for breaking the tie?

I'd say "What the hell!" and give up,
but when I cock my hat and head recklessly
to the left like a frontispiece Walt Whitman,
he tilts his to the right like the young
and questing James Joyce on the Liffey Bridge!

Mel Kneels Down in the Confessional Beside Bill and Carl

> *hog in sloth, fox in stealth, wolf in greediness,*
> *dog in madness, lion in prey.*
> —WM. SHAKESPEARE

> *There is a wolf in me . . . fangs pointed for tearing*
> *gashes . . . a red tongue for raw meat . . . and*
> *the hot lapping of blood—I keep the wolf because*
> *the wilderness will not let it go . . .*
> *I got a menagerie inside my ribs, under my bony head,*
> *under my red valve heart . . .*
> —CARL SANDBURG

Well, boys, it's a zoo here too!
There's a mess of owls and skunks
in my timber, and noises

that'll keep a camper awake!
I'm an ark full of grunting and baying.

Noah never heard such a din.
We didn't come just from wilderness,
but from something older and blacker.
We rooted deep in a cornucopia
that still hasn't stopped spilling its stars.

The snake and I
were among the first stuff spit

like a cork from the astral bung.
We rode here on the tail of a bronco
comet waving our hats.

Every summer the snake and I writhe
and chafe our way out of last year's skin.
Folks swear it's a fine fit, but if
I can't slough it, I'll die.

I have a crow in me who thinks he's a lark.
He can't hit a note, but longs to sing
at heaven's gate. Worse than any magpie,
he loves his squawk. Words are seeds
for his beak to crack. Each yields him
a kernel to cackle. Nothing is too black
for him to contemplate with his piss-yellow eye.
The crow and I came from a long-ago
sneeze of the stars. It was we
who made the black hole black.

I have a fox in me
that can smell a female
miles away; my nose can track her
down the center of a creek; double cross
or loop her trail as she will, she can't
shake me—it is I who circle ahead
and spread my allure, and behind a log
watch her puzzle and sniff
my scatter of flattery
and praise, every best word
about loveliness and the shine
of her hair, until at last

she will have to come to me
and admit I have the most
elegant tail in the woods.

I have a pig in me who farts his way
through slops of macaroni and cheese,
and a moose with a hardon like a misplaced antler.
The moose and the pig and I came from sputum
hawked from the throat of a star.

There's a weasel in me, albino
and cowardly blind, weaving and ducking
along ditches, ready to hide
behind every stump of an excuse,
avoiding my friends like enemies, wanting
only a narrow hole full of my own smell
to worm into, where I can sleep behind
a fake snarl, my butt against the back wall,
my teeth bared toward the door.

After the first cosmic blaze snuffled out,
I and the weasel wriggled up anemic
out of the pale ashpile.

I have a hound in me who howled all night
the day my friend died, howled with such
a wavering howl that leaves fell from the trees
and neighbors nightmared in their sleep.
The hound and I were the last broken-tailed stuff
scraped from the cooling caves of fire.

But all of these things are not as strange
as the other things I need to confess.

In a world perforated with gunfire
and darkened with lies, I still feel
stirrings of other stuff got from the stars.

Though I wade knee-deep in toxins
through landfills of stress

many days there is a porpoise in me, effortlessly arcing
out of the sea. And some mornings a butterfly
leaps up in the light and hangs between geranium
and hollyhock unable to decide. There are days
when a mockingbird inside rarely pauses
in his blissful recitals, and a hawk
climbs on spirals of wind, high up, until he can see
everything, every hunched mouse, its one
exposed whisker, all of it, with a perfect eye.

Climbing in the Lake Country

Carrying nothing, traveling light, free
and alone in the great world, I start
at first dawn up the foot trail to Helm Crag.
Behind me, Grasmere sleeps and falls away,
the lake rippling her skin under a chill wind.
In the next valley Ullswater opens
a bright eye to the rising sun; halfway
up the near range, Easdale Tarn
rings her silver echo, and Sour Milk Gill
spills bright floss into the valley.

When at last I pull myself up,
clinging, to the tip of the crag,
the sun winks hot and cold
from quick clouds and the wind
burnishes and wakes the flesh.

Far below sheep are confetti
on the fields, gulls flare and fall
like thrown salt where an early tractor
crawls a corduroy of windrowed hay.

Ringing outward in a rumple of hills
and polished lakes, the land glories
green and silver, and tiny high tarns
sprinkle pizzicato to the soft
symphony of space and light.

Suddenly stripping my clothes away, I catch
the last scarce toehold on the narrow peak
and stand up
in cold
wind and
bright sun
naked
I am

III.

RELIGHTING THE LAMP

Bavarian Bees

The bees of Bavaria must have started that rumor—
that stuff about the busyness of bees I mean.

They sizzle out over a land so blistered
by bloom, they have no time to bumble or loll.
It has to be for them a quick-in and a quick-out
of the cannas and callas, the ubiquitous
window boxes of geraniums, the fence rows
of jasmine and iris, buttercup and salvia.
They are mad shoppers in red and blue spills
of Christmas candy quick-marts; they careen
the streets of the dahlias klaxoning like Nazis;
there is hysteria in the crepe myrtle and hibiscus.

But flowers are only cheap, low-grade drugs
for addicts so crazed by the world's sweetness.
Wild for harder stuff, they invade
grocery stores like renegade panzers, sucking
at the soft ends of bananas, circumambulating
the puzzling hide of Snickers bars, drinking
from the broken breasts of cantalopes,
the wet vulvas of burst plums.
In garbage dumpsters full of Coke cups
their noise revs to a race car whine;
in restaurants they snowshoe across
whipped creams, tipple at the brink of wine glasses,
climb the strudel. In a world of bright confections
they are insatiable to have it all, to save

it for home, for the incredible banks
of honeycomblove stored somewhere golden
in the hollows of sycamores or the splayed
ends of discarded brandy barrels.

Bavarians, having lived forever with such madness,
are blind to it, deaf, placid, indulgent.
There is no swatting or shooing or even
leaning away from this perpetual presence.
Bees and people ignore one another, inches apart.

But in strangers, the bees are interested.
Jaded by native Rieslings and roses
they look into the red mouths
and blue eyes of tourists;
they curl like question marks
hunkering to hang themselves
into the curved petals of our ears.

Is it something we wear, or use
in our wash? Or is it that our eyes
still see them, our ears still hear?

I think they must be looking for some flower
never yet found, some last nectar
and ultimate bloom, but why do they
damnably assume and hang before my face
like inverted commas around an unspoken space?
My tongue is stammerer, not stamen;
I awake to my nectarless eyes.

What do they want from my mouth?
What do they want me to say?
That I am stung by their quizzing?
That in a world lush with sun and the juices
of giving, I have spoken no adequate sweetness?
That I shall henceforth no longer stumble hollow
among the pollens of living without
hiving something in the heart
like honeyed light.

Facing the Light

1. Van Gogh: the Work

In small doses, Van Gogh fascinates,
but too much of him scalds,
alters our eyes, skins us raw
to serpent fear and the tactics
of sun in intense terrains
of schizoid light.

Landscapes undulate and break
like seas, green trees
crackle and burn, the cat ignites
electric and white hot,
clouds boil with limitless god,
and the air smokes swirling away
from the shoulders of things,
things shuddering to be more
than themselves.

If only any thing would stand still,
if only the light would lie down,
if only the straw would stay put,
the colors cool and be spent
like the sleepers in the noon
haystack, but everywhere in the torn
field the paint stubble leaps up
like splashed rain, and light chitters madness
and madness, pizzicatoes faster and faster

toward the horizons, fleeing away
from the stacked straw that bulges
and pulses toward flashpoint
of unbearable and hideous praise.

2. VAN GOGH: THE PLACE
In the south of France, rolling for miles along
the trafficless cool shady gravelly white macadam
through stately blonde lines of old sycamores,
I come suddenly out into the bright open, the sun
generous among the roadside dill, alive
on the Languedoc fields tipping at all angles
to the horizons, and I see the light
that drove Van Gogh mad, and feel unaccountable joy.

Maybe it is only for a few moments that such light cleanses
and then, prolonged, would push us, too, to writhing
sanities and insane clarities. But here, now, it lifts
for this moment, all that is not clear, leaves only
itself, and the knock of joy that breaks my throat.

Confessing Addiction

1. Early Abuse

From youngest memory, I was hooked.
My parents never guessed the dangers
that lay in the luminous world
where they pushed me to work and play.
They let me wander the lanes
where light was for sale
and sun was easy to score.
They never thought to protect me
from the ten thousand purveyors
of ten thousand varieties of shine.

My mother should never have allowed
me out in the glare of the snow
to leap up for the icicles alive
in the sun along the smokehouse eaves.
I should not have been asked
to scatter the gold shelled corn
among white flurries of pullets,
or permitted to stand beneath the mulberry
and watch the wind's shellgame
shifting leaves green and berries
red and blue-black.
                              My eyes
might have been spared the bright
duel between the barn's tin roof
and the sun, that old eye-for-an-eye

and tooth-for-a-tooth of furious light.

And *how could* my father, after the corn
was shucked and the hay all in,
have abandoned me and let me fish
a whole afternoon while the low-arcing
October sun on the ripples chipped
and chipped its divots of gold
into my eyes until I was lost,
carried away, and the whole pond
became for me one giant fish
spanking his scales in the sun.

2. A Second Substance

Like every child at first, I was afraid
of the dark. Years later I discovered
her long-neglected allure, the midnight
fire and the passion, and explored
like Milton's Lucifer the wide kingdoms
of the visible dark. Since then I have sung
soft songs to darkness, swum
in its swift torrents, navigated deep
into the Congo of my animal psyche,
dancing and howling on the shore.

3. Schizophrenic Episodes

For a time, confused and torn, I was angry
at the great blond God who had seemed
for centuries to claim for his light
shows all the glory, old Nobodaddy
cracking his lightnings like Oz.

4. CONVALESCENCE

But now I see it was never a cosmic war
of dark and light, but our slavish
historical fear of them both, our puritan taste
for gray.
          Everywhere the cosmos is at love,
a black and white intercourse, blaze and soot,
the bruise-black sky full of stars, not haze.

Darkest passions flourish best in tropical sun.
When we made love in a canoe on the Amazon,
the bottom silt stirred with thrashing piranha.
Fondle this flesh in a field of ripening wheat
and thunder will roll black and unfettered beneath us.
And who has seen more light than hovers above us
in the black rooms of our blackest love?

5. FAILING THERAPY

Though I love the dark as well as light,
still I have no talent for hiding in caves.
I'm nothing like a newt. My father wasn't
a bat. In these windowless corporate offices
my ram's horn crumples, everything shrivels and pits
like drying morels, or sops down to the black ooze
of aging inkycaps. Without honest light, my words
moulder rank and blue, like leather in damp basements.
I couldn't be a coal-miner, or develop photos
in an infra-red lab. Don't send me application blanks
to become a Carlsbad Cavern guide. I won't last
as a movie critic. English fog pushes me, too,
to stick my head in an oven; too much
Irish mist and I want to fling myself in the bog

as ritual sacrifice. Shroud all funerals
that I am to take seriously in heavy draperies,
but eventually turn me loose in the sun.

I can survive these windowless rooms for a while
on artificial fluorescence; the incandescent bulb
can keep me barely alive: but in short space
I've got to have fire, got to have light.

I can stand an evening or two of candlelight,
your perfume curling toward me across the *pate,*
unravelling the strands of my DNA; I relish
with you these few hot hours lit only
by the red numerals of the bedside digital clock.
But soon I must have skylights. Give me high windows,
give me the Kansas plains. No less
than 360 degrees of horizon will do.

6. RELAPSE
I'm hooked. My mother should never have showed me
to the moon. She should not have asked me to stoke
the fire beneath the black cauldron of homemade soap
in a backyard full of sun where the horse-mower blades
were cocked up and flashed in the light
like Lucifer's teeth, where the horses drinking
from the water trough stirred with their muzzles
those undulating lozenges of light, where
the roosters' lush combs flushed translucent and red,
and against the clothesline post, the oystershell chat
for the hens spilled from the slashed sack, all broken
and iridescent in the sun.

7. Facing Up

I envy those Eskimos the linguists claimed
had thirty-two words for the varieties of snow.

Can the numen be named? I seldom say
anything bright. I lack the sun's
lexicon. My diction is light.

Words for My Father
Who Gave Me Space Instead

Your German name exempted you
from love talk; but a man, without saying
anything, can leave a gap beside him.

Because I was not the center
of your world, I could stand up in it,
an untaught learner, a boy witnessing
what a man does, must do. It was space
neither of us had to rent with words

or anything else we didn't have.

If I had to choose for you one stance,
I would stand you in the evening heat
looking to the west over the withering
corn, reading the wisp of cloudbank
that would or would not blow up rain,
and I already reading your shoulders,
their dropped angles.
                        You never spoke
those weights, never packed
for me a bag of stones.
The boy in me listens still,
learning a man's silences.

How My Father Milked

In my father's quick, experienced hands
the cows leaned into the stanchions
in a trance of ecstasy, letting
their milk down. His bowed head
unmoving against the cow's side,
on his forearms the muscles
rode up and down like pistons,
arms stroking like the drivers
on a locomotive, the milk boiling
into the bucket even a little like
the rhythm of a steam engine
at full throttle, the billowing
foam rising above the rim,
the paired streams switching angles
like the legs of a man running, a man
running for his life, faster and faster,
running not to fall on his face,
running to keep a house and farm
from falling,from falling,from falling

Loading Prairie Hay

Standing today in the sun on the ripening
newly-cut lawn, I see larger fields,
and my father in them; smell the waft
of meadows, alfalfa, lespedeza, sweet
clover, oatgrass, foxtail, brome.

Where the sulky rake
has dumped the windrowed hay
in humps, his pitchfork tucks up
loose timothy, then bites and takes
the whole shock, hefting it
in one high sweep to me on the rack.

His fork goes back once
to glean the scattered wisps
and turn them up to the load
like a handful of loose change.

Before the horses can start the load,
or I step up through the hay
—or quit this dream—
he is halfway to the next haycock
his shouldered fork flashing
sharp tines at the sun.

When he sets the fork again,
he will turn to look back
at the world he has lifted up
and me riding on its top.

Waste Not, Want Not

Let Gary Snyder brag about the Shoshone
or the Iroquois, how they wasted nothing,
used every antler and hoof, made wampum
bags of bladders, jewelry from teeth.
On our Kansas farm, pure German, and poor,
we didn't have to take lessons from Indians,
nor hire landfills for trash. We saved it all,
old wire, scraps of tin, broken handles, each thing
kept until the day it would rise again in glorious
and unpredictable resurrection, as something else,
pigeon coop, tomato stake, whatever a farmer's
imagination suddenly recognized
it had been waiting to be.

Even the mulberry stump stayed on twenty years,
living its afterlife as a chopping block, stuccoed
with feathers and hatchet scars. The rooster
himself, his loose head yawning and gapping there
on the black altar momentarily, before the dog
snatched and cracked it in his toothy smile,
could count on being entirely consumed, his guts
to be argued between the hogs and hounds,
his feathers to fatten the garden compost,
and we to eat every bit of the rest,
and make soup of the bones. Mom didn't have
to hide the giblets in gravy: we could look
a gizzard in the eye. Even the skinned feet
came to the table, in a separate dish

hooking their three-fingered fists
in a slurry of flour and broth. And
sometimes after supper, Mom would look
at me as if I'd forgotten something,
and I'd go out to the back porch, stand
on the edge of the step, flap my elbows,
and crow.

Lighting the Lamp

Long ago on the open prairies, nights
stretched out full and heavy
like black bears sleeping
oblivious to the sting
of the high mosquito stars.

And even in the Kansas of my boyhood,
for miles the night's hide lay unpunctured.
Our chores and milking finished,
we sat under the cedars,
waiting for the house to cool,
while jet blotted the barn
and inked away the west.
Cicadas and crickets had already
polished the dark to a sheen
before we found our way lightless to bed.
We slept quietly in its deep black hand.

It was altogether different in winter,
when early dusk frightened us
to the kitchen where Mom worked on
in a darkening house; we hungered
wordlessly for the lighting of the lamp,
for the flare of the sulphur
match and the leap of shadows, her own
looming on the wall behind her
as she touched the wick aflame.
The smell of kerosene, and the long wait

for the Aladdin mantle to warm,
before she eased the flame up
and a glow pushed outward into the room.
Like chicks to a hen, we drew
under the skirt of our mother's light.
Now the dark could only crouch
behind the woodbox. Upstairs
it waited, though, in a cold room
where later we would have to climb,
lifting high only the candle's
tiny trembling umbrella.

When we were older, a greater fear
was the winter dark that hunkered outside
where we might be called upon to walk
with swinging lantern alongside
our huge striding and scissoring shadow
to a barn full of beasts and cats'eyes.

A hundred kinds of Kansas dark
taught me all the stories of light.

Which I forget. Now. Here. Almost.
Under this fluorescent glare.

Tonight, at the edges of cities, darkness sniffs
like a small furred animal, hesitates—
and dreaming only a thin ghost of itself
forward through the alleys, it cringes
in yard corners and cowers under cars waiting
to mewl with a slight and domesticated dark
tossed out from the houses with the flick of a wrist.

Hounded by instant incandescence, it breeds
nervously, is nearly extinct. Reclusive
and odorless, no one has noted it for years.

Having lost touch with darkness
we ourselves grow shadowy and weightless.
Taking the light too lightly
our bones grow birdlike, and we threaten
to float unmoored from the earth.

But the gravity that pulls me back, like weights
in my shoes, is memory, and how the immense dark
backed from the bright circle spreading
from my mother's hands on the lamp.

Watching My Mother's Breath

for Regina Mersmann (Oct. 15, 1899–Aug. 28, 1990)

For hours after the stroke
you were like a house being closed;
one after one the blinds came down.

Now on this high bed, your face
says death, but your heart clings
to an old habit; you
have not been here for days.

You sleep and sleep, as if to sleep
for all those nights waking
with children in the cold house.

I put drops in your eyes, swab
your dry, gaping mouth with a sponge,
say to you the few things we would not
have known how to listen to together.

Beyond washboard and breadboard now,
your thin body is pulled
into the sheets by an immense
and eloquent fatigue. Will you
have to sleep for years
before you can go on ahead?

In unmistakeable stages your breathing
alters; sometimes stumbles, and stops—
then, comes again, weaker
from a deepening cave.

90 years of sand hurries from the hour-
glass back toward its first ocean.

In you now the breath backs slowly away,
bowing, toward the wings; the flame
wavers smaller and smaller,
re-entering the ember.

All those years of gardens
arrange themselves in the palm
of your hand.

In the root cellar, potatoes
settle shoulder to shoulder;
the rock weighing down
the plate on the kraut jar falls
more deeply asleep.

Time moves away down the walk, waving goodbye.

In your ears, violin cases wrap themselves
shut over the gleaming wood;
chairs are being stacked
and leaned against the wall.

In your mouth the table is cleared
for the last time, the floors
swept and shining.

Your sleep slides deeper,
your breath rocking you lower
and lower into your self, back

through the rings within rings
to the hut in the woods where
the master takes your head in his hands
smiling at your perfection;
and leads you to the hearth
where you crawl into the fire,
and the sky opens its hand,
full of stars, and the wren's eye
looks out bright from the hole
of her small house.

IV.

Dusting
the Reliquary

Mel Divides the Waters

When I rev the Evinrude to an airplane whine,
the boat's bow noses up like an airliner
and my wake razors the lake's belly wide,
unzipping the water's smooth skin,
rolling it open in long white rows.

I am flying in catfish sky
laying contrail for bass
opening a schism
in wall-eye theology
stirring The Awakening
in parishes of perch.

At some level I
make perfect sense.
This roaring is *logos,*
my circlings are signs.

It doesn't matter if
I'm going anywhere;
I'm going there quick,
and I'm leaving a track.

Mel Prunes His Flowers

Until they make seed, they bloom,
showing off their charms, pulling in
the thighs of bees until their pistils
are sleeked with pollen. Fertilized,
they fade. Successful loveliness pales.
Petals drooping limp and uncombed,
they puff matronly with seed.

Still tight in the bud, their virgin
sisters quit growing, cloistering
like nuns in their locked sepals.

Shall I let motherhood and chastity
drain the world of color?

In rebellion, my hand rises:
when the blush faints on rose
or zinnia, and before any pod
can swell like a belly, I behead
them like Henry's wives. Unabashed

I am an aborter of rose hips,
the undertaker of spent bloom.
I do the work of jackals, hyenas:
I slice a fat world lean.
Like a vulture, I snatch
the old bone clean.

If I am a brute,
it is for brightness.
Whatever you think of me
and my steel hand, it is
such love that lures all
the bright young Lolitas
out of their chaste frocks.

My garden is blood red
with flirtation and curtsying.

Oh, I am beauty's bully!
I pimp for bees.

Starting Toward Damascus,
Paul Was a Tourist, Too

The tourists take turns in London's St. Paul's
posing for snapshots at the communion rail.
Their stance is stiff and cold against the warm
golds and greens of the nave, the windows'
yellows and blues. Beneath Sir Christopher's
great canopied narthex, they adjust
their glasses, fix collars, and are annoyed
when others stray into the camera's path.
Their pose says "Here I am at St. Paul's"—

In their albums a hundred pictures
likewise shall attest: "Here I am
at Buckingham Palace," "Here I am
at Stonehenge," "Here I am
at the Taj Mahal," and "Here I am
at the Louvre." "And that,
by the Matterhorn, is me." Always
the megalithic stones, the pyramids,
the massive architecture dwarfing
tiny figures gussied in Gucci.

Above them here in St. Paul's,
Wren's arches sing *Benedicite*
Omnia Opera Domini Domino,
Omnes Bestiae et Pecora,
Omnia Quae Moventur in Aquis,
Omnes Volvares Coeli.

Oh, blessed be all the works
of the Lord! All the beasts
and fishes, all that moves
in water, and flies in air!

And blest be the tourists who
move in chartered boats and planes,
tour buses, and rented cars,
ferries and trains, horse shays
and gondolas, rickshaws, camel
back, and ass back,
                                carrying
their "I ams" like tiny icons,
standing unstricken
by all that is
magnificent and grand.

On First Seeing Michelangelo's David in the Stone

The guidebook warns he is not
anatomically perfect, his thighs
too short, his head too large.

When I see him, I am lightning struck
with love and envy, my knees feel
impotence before witnessed power.
If I were a woman, I would die for this boy.

He is looking across his shoulder
toward a Goliath only he can see.
If there is a remnant of a smile
it is leftover from the moment
when the crowd shouted "Dahveed! Dahveed!
Dahveed!" and he could first see the giant
folly of confronting the world's insanity.

His sling he hooks over his shoulder
with two fingers, the way Peter Falk
would carry his raincoat, or James Dean
his jacket entering a dance hall;
in his other hand he grips the stone
like a split-fingered slider.

He knows he is a rookie facing a rout,
and his whole body is beautiful with reluctance.

Moving the Snake

The grackles in their black cassocks believe,
rocking and chirring in grand gestures
from the fenceposts. But the jays
in the privet are skeptical and scold
the over-sized plastic snake riding high
among the ripening figs. They are tired of choking
down shrivelled hackberries; they've had a crawful
of thistle and pigweed. They jeer, but keep their distance.

The snake glitters in the sun. His eyes never blink.
He is looped and coiled indifferently,
like a tax man on lunch break,
but his mouth and tongue
smile wide-red and personal.

The robin on the lawn listens stoically to the fescue,
pretending by his cocked head, he is oblivious
to sybaritic appetites, loves only the bitter
cricket and grimed worm. But his up-eye cannot blink
the laden tree and its snaky fruit.

A titmouse, his own eyes bulging like figs,
checks in to the nearby cedar—and is gone off quick
as a teenager in a whorehouse.

All day from surrounding box elders, the birds
preach and argue. Lust and deny.
Crowds of thrush, sparrow and chickadee,

cowbird and starling have statements to make.

Each night, wearing the monkish cowl
of dark, I climb the branches,
and move the snake, alter his attitudes.
Each day the birds renew their seriousness
and miss the fruitless irony: I have
taught the snake to say "Thou shalt not!"

The figs pend purple and full, untouched.

All the figs are mine!

The Dogs of War

(the week before "Desert Storm")

The midnight racket rakes me out of sleep,
a hubbub like wrecked cars in a blender,
hell-broke-loose in the suburbs, Navajos
or Baptists at war, the rapture with gongs.
Outside the fence three neighborhood strays
bark and leap, dancing in snarling synchrony
with my Husky and Lab on the inside, all five
in a paroxysm, at full voice, raging
and threatening like TV wrestlers, teeth
and spittle, snap and slaver, crowding
the wire. How brave and perfect

each is, how full of the joy of ferocity,
ready to tear the enemy, untiring, sure
of God and war, far from thought of turning
tail-between-the-legs. Their sincerity

depends upon a chain-link fence.

Safe and uncut, they love the bite
of words, the rippling of muscles unripped.
Until we bleed under the long tooth,
feel the hot mouth of death close
at our throats, we are warriors all.

Frantic and immune they bark on, tearing
up the terrace in storms of zoysia and slobber.
They might continue forever

except that suddenly the God-who-loves-sleep
blazes on the porch: "Get the Hell Out of Here,
You God-Damned Dirty Mongrel Sons-a-Bitches!"

Quick and low the three are across the street,
looking over their shoulders.
My two wheel panting toward the house
and pirouette on the steps to be petted—
as if they have defended something.

Lapsarian Hummingbirds

I've hung feeders at every corner
of the house—replenished, infinite
wells—intending each hummer to savor
long serene draughts of pure gift.

But all the drinking done here is furtive
and quick, stolen between sneak and flinch.
Every feeder is disputed. No bird drinks
without some ferocious hypodermic
exploding from a lookout stob,
some brother kamikaze flinging
toward him like a tavern dart.
When five or six get to jousting
at once, there's such buzz and blur
and flashings past with the sound *thrroat*
and then again *thrroat* the other way,
the feeder glows like a nucleus
orbited by furious electrons.

Well, if they can't see
how hurtful all this is
to hummingbird economy, how they
burn more gas than they can retank
between skirmishes; if they can't see
that the nectar always returns,
inexhaustible, that each red feeder
has flowers for four
where they could sit down together

like Mafia in an Italian restaurant—
well, it's no use preaching to them
about loaves and fishes. Why did I
suppose anyone coming with such red bibs
could learn to smile and sip
their sop like the very hogs of Plato?

Pond Politics

In the backyard lily pond,
goldfish not necessarily gold
spawned hundreds of fry, fizzing the water
with their small ecstasies. Red on white,
ink on orange, leopards, pickled blondes,
and hordes of nondescript gray-blacks.

The bright ones shimmer and flash
in grey-green water; the dark ones
disappear as shadows under the sheen.
Clearly too many fish for a small pond,
and all grown big enough for bait.

With a fine net I scoop them up,
returning technicolors to the pond,
ticking the dark fry into the bait pail.
Confused in the white bucket, they flicker
like an old movie. A *film noire*,
perhaps, with me as the villain. Well,
it's true, I'm the wrong God for them.
I see too much with my eyes.

With a hook through their lips, they may
be of some use to my other senses,
to the kinetics of catgut, the sizzle,
and smell of filets in the skillet.

The Jungian in me squirms,
and the liberal winces.

But I doubt whether it's darkness
that's at risk, nor gender or race.
Still, this matter of beauty may be
somewhat too narrowly conceived.

Listen, ordinarily I'm delighted
when poems climb out of their pond
to swim in larger waters, but
not this one. Couldn't we
just agree the lake is full
of teeth, and these are
fish rites and nothing more?

Misplacing the Modifier:
or "Understanding the Rocks in Your Head"

How could it be I'd never gotten word
    among all the Riviera talk I'd heard?
Beaches from *Nice* up to *Cannes*
    haven't got a speck of sand!
Bathers come in a flock,
    but they content themselves with rock:
pebbles that roll and slide
    at the whimsy of the tide.
Here the surf again, and once more,
    throws the gravel up the shore,
and where the bank is steep,
    the rocks chatter and seem to speak
when, after their briny ride,
    they, falling back, collide.

But what it is they spell,
    neither Frost nor I would tell.
"Misery" was the whispered word
    that Matthew Arnold elsewhere heard:
a muddled ebb and flow
    swirling history's tragic undertow.
Poor Matthew had the shingles
    thinking the world unfit for singles!
But both he and Wordsworth hurried;
    poetically and publicly they worried
for the myths and juices reason stole
    from failing nature's dying soul.

But Frost and I (notice that I wink)
    do not propose nor think
it's any human knowing
    that keeps the cosmos going,
nor that nature's so human or so small
    as to speak to us at all.
And yet these rolling stones
    sing with such insistent tones
and repeated crashing lyrics—
    are such clackings empty pyrrhics?

It surely seems like treason
    to think rock rhymes without reason,
or believe all this salty palaver
    is only trivial boulder dash and blather.

Today with the world up for hire,
    the rocks should be saying the fat is in the fire,
morally proclaiming the bared breast
    is sure sign of the declining West;
part of their Riviera pitch
    should be some sort of sass against the rich.

But if rock means by rolling, or wisely refrains,
    at least to me stone never explains.
I know absolutely, though, the sound that it makes
    when down from the bank it scrabbles and rakes:
that furious hot sizzle and excitement of grease
    when bacon is dropped in by the piece.

I roll over, easy, listen and listen.

     The stones scramble, sputter, and glisten.

Whether I, or Frost, hear rocks in a rush,
     or audition a scythe (that speaks with a hush),
if there is sun (or a star) to take,
     we leave words, and the hay, to make.

Whatever its source or its ground,
     it's with the wordless word and its sound
that Frost and I are taken.
     Oh, may the divine and speechless sea
forever fry for me
     rashers and rashers of bacon!

Dusting the Reliquary

That wild Baptist, John, may have lost his head,
But such things get found, my friends.
It may be a little unsound (and apparently dead),
But we still have it around, at Amiens.

Any of us, if we're human, are apt to collect stuff:
String, or coins, or ivory-inlaid boxes for snuff.
But in a wide world of finders-keepers and philatelics,
Holy Mother Church is surely Queen of the Relics.
(What other collector comes so close to Perfection,
Or has more skill at increasing the collection?)

For centuries churchmen have had it by heart:
the Virgin never, not ever, lost her maiden's hood.
At the thought they grow pale. To think that she could!
Mary wasn't a tart!
Yet somebody got away with her veil—
We have it at Chartres.

Christ was born in a stone stall of a stone stable,
Yet the Crusaders were incredibly able
(at no risk to their rank, but some spiritual danger),
To bring home more than one plank from the manger.
Go to Rome, and you can adore a board (and divine *cacciatore*).
We keep the best in an urn at *la chiesa da Santa Maria Maggiore.*

And from the Cross, as we certainly should,
We also have a good bit of the wood.

If you've been a good giver,
You may already own you a sliver.
As for nails, if twenty is plenty,
We have enough, and of other stuff—
No need to count thorns, we have extras.
(If it's a matter of crowns, we're ambidextrous!)

We may be Procrustian, but we're not procrastian:
We have the arrows of St. Sebastian,
The chains of St. Lawrence, to say nothing of Pete,
The Evangelist's jaw, and Bartholomew's sheet.
We've got the hip of St. Mark, a chip off the block of St. Luke,
And, to prove it wasn't a fluke, besides the Baptist's head,
We've got some fingers and toes and the bones of his nose,
And his belt, it's a cinch (though probably not more than an inch),
And such other disciple-trifle and apostle-ossify on hand,
We could make and dress us a man.
Of Abraham, Isaac, and Jacob, we have personal sand.

And though I haven't seen it yet,
I'm confidently sure (and willing to bet):
Somewhere kept in a golden cup
Must be a petrified turd picked up
From the hooves of the donkey whose breathing
Kept the blood in the manger from freezing—
And it is thus that many Christians in mass
Are blessed with the understanding of an ass.

Tarantula

(Forked Mountain—Ouachita National Forest)

My wrong shoes slip on the steep trail.
Sliding and floundering between boulders
I pull myself upward, fearing the long
zigzagging carom down the mountain.

Just yards from the peak, in a cleft
where I must crawl, a tarantula
almost the size of my hand, eye-to-eye.
Two trucks meeting on a narrow bridge.
I stare at his calm, high-legged stance.
There is time to consider this.

My father would have smashed him
unthinking, the way he killed
most small things, stomping the iridescent
beetle, hoeing the snake in the hempweeds,
echoing his fathers, good-man-blind.

But somehow the killer in me's gotten disconnected.
It was the spider's territory. I had not
been summoned. Still I wanted
the top whistling with wind
where the sun blazed and the gods waited
and the vistas circled mile beyond mile
over the ridges. All other route leaned out
over the precipice. Could I outwait him?

Did he ever go elsewhere?

Neither of us could know
that, in the end, I would take off
my shoes, and ease my weight up and out
onto the exposed ledge, belly-crawling
like a postulant where stones skittered
down and away to the valley below.

And so for a while we waited there
on the mountain, while the wilderness
hung around us, and tufts of wind
lifted strands of his long hair-shirt,
contemplating one another,
I and one of the gods
I had not known
I had come for.

V.

Born Again
of Woman
and the Flesh

Woman, Not Praised Enough

When God, or Nature, or simple Chance
made all things, he made you last.
After practice, after trial and change,
finding the colors, the shapes,
the melodies that lift, the grace
of sunlit waves, light fit
for the blade of your thigh risen
to loaved buttock and butter of waist,
back soft with sinews and white slopes,
sculpted shoulder, delicate hollows
of collar bone, and the neck's long silk
up the bared throat to the open ear,
that quaver of breath drawn in
that goads a man's blood to rise.

Whoever the artificer, he learned
at the hummingbird's throat before
trying the blaze of your fierceness;
at the dawn's pinks before choosing
the orgasmic flush of your neck.
Ocean storms modeled your motions
of love; long slow rains the loll
and long silence afterwards.

Love Song

Tonight Orion muscles his light across the South
like a mindless bully of hope, and the moon
smiles like a Shulamite, dangling
a jeweled foot from a hammock of gold.

All the heavens are black and comely, the night
air clean as a flute run; everywhere buds
push against their green locks, and I die
remembering your loveliness, gone these long years
like a comet far beyond sight, spinning
always farther away, and as impossible to recall.
What shall I do with the leftover magnificence,
Aprils full of marsh wrens and wild iris, days
when even the gravel gleams, and my heart
is a kicked hole in my chest.

Valentine

Woman dimming in the distance,
so many years gone. Once in my life
you were thunderstorm and lightning,
downpour and surging flood, symphonic
music whanging the rafters, forest fire
flaring from bracken to treetops.
There was room for nothing else: you reached
from horizon to horizon like a Yukon white-out,
a whole hemisphere of hurricane.
And when you were gone, your weather
hung on, swept me day after day.

Today the landscape is stormless.
Slowly as an eroding mountain, a climate shifting,
you have been leaving me bit by bit, diminishing
in the distance. Each day, like a drying lake,
I grow smaller, hold less
and less of the disappearing sky.
At night sometimes, the last loon,
resisting departure,
rises on the waters
and lifts his solitary call.

Naples

In a sidewalk cafe in the impossible heat
of noon, I drink blessedly icy beer
and swallow the intense color and motion
of the street, the swarm of language and flesh:
swarthy open-shirted pedestrians pushing
through the tables, brushing the wide-brimmed
hats of customers; the muscled busboy
moving swiftly in white tee shirt
and dark curls; the deft-handed waiter
in a soiled jacket carrying food
arranged like art for the eye;
the ignored curbside vendor, arms akimbo
enduring in big-stomached breaths
beside his blackening bananas;
shopkeepers propped in doorways
along sun-baked sidewalks, litter-strewn,
piss-streaked; starved dogs so crippled
none of their legs touch the ground;
a fruit-rind "soccer ball" resting
in the gutter while its urchins argue and eat
in mother-loud walk-ups, laundry
festooning all the high windows;
the sun, the sun, beating, pressing;
and suddenly—like everywhere Latin
on this beautiful, tormenting planet—
a wonderfully breasted *donna*
in hotly bunched clothes,
heading somewhere,

high-heeled,
eyes asmoke,
stirring a musk breeze,
the last delicate hairs at the nape
curling up with sweat.

Six Portraits of Magdalene

Titian
Of course, there is his golden light
on her flesh. She is listening, a little,
partly hearing the chastisement,
but her eyes are far away with the mystery.
Her hands cradle her hair,
not covering but adorning her breasts
in glorious haloes, tresses just
browner than nipples. She will be ready
with a remark to make him laugh
when his sermon is done.

Ludovico Cigoli
All of this darkness, Maggie! That skull
by your side! There is hardly light enough
to see your hand and the clutched book. It is
too small to be the Pentateuch. Is it his
testament, always new? His song?

Anonymous
Maudlin, not-pretty, broad butted,
alone, black hair in a black cave
dissolving into black cloud. Your body
faintly shines like a newt, beyond light.
But no, breaking the black in the high
left—there—pale, almost invisible lightfall.
You are moonflesh. Reflective.

Guido Cagnacci ("Magdalena Portata en Cielo")
How strange, Magdalena, that the artist—
and thus God—gives you, too, the carnival ride
straight up through the clouds. Not baroque
marshmallow bouffant clouds, but healthy
stormless El Greco. And above, heaven
is not light, but dark turbulence
and thrusting excitement. Gowned only
in your hair, your hips almost hide
the lucky lifting angel. Trailing an olive leg,
you rise like a woman approaching a lover, breasts
pushing up through brown waterfalls of hair.

Donatello, Wood Sculpture
This is wrong and unfair! It cannot be
true, this New York bag woman
mourning her sins, this skinsack
of sagging and joyless bones. Her matted
hair is hairshirt, the beast shag
of the desert baptist. Not sin, not
even sorrow for a gone Christ could sink
such cheeks and eyes. Loved perfectly once,
in a woman some bloom keeps; no such grief
or guilt ever rode the wake of a lord.
His absence is possible, but not
the fire of his connection, his savor.
Her nostrils keep the flare of his iron
odors. And she does not repent. The body
of a loved woman does not forget,
and rides forever like a light boat
on the swell of a redeemed past.

Rodin, WHITE MARBLE

Stone turned flesh, Magdalen hangs
on the cross with Christ; her left hand
holds on where his right is nailed.
Her body leans down and across
to kiss him on his clean and unmarked left side,
on that sensitive spot, high and just
inside the left hip, his left shoulder shuddering
down at the light touch of her lips just there
where he is so alive. His head is thrown back,
eyes rolled, mouth open. His tied hands strain
to reach down, want so to reach down, to caress
the hair of her head, the head of the mouth
that kisses so lightly there,
to feel the hard wonder of her skull
like a small melon in his cupped hands.
He does not doubt the resurrection to come,
nor does any man if he be born again
of woman and the flesh. This last great death
so like all the little deaths,
his power dying into the world's flesh,
his spine dissolving into light.

Notre Dame D'Amiens

In the great church of Notre Dame d'Amiens,
noon light slants clean as flute song,
but the organ's music darkens and climbs,
swirling and falling, looming up, breaking
itself on its own burlyings, until the perfect
verticals of stone must wish to leap and turn
in the grand clean symmetries of vaulted space.

In the organ storm, among tourists,
a tall blonde, lithe as a taper,
wanders the great floor. Her eyes
drink at the spaces. I see how
her feet, turning, taste the stone;
how her young dancer's body aches to leap
and pirouette where everything lifts
and arcs open in echoing light.

Oh Marie, Marie, come back tonight
when the city sleeps, and find
by the grace of god the door unlocked;
and entering in, your slow steps echoing
cold and high in the froth of clerestory
moonlight, take the center and let go.

In your white clothes dance like a dervish
in the wingsilk light; let your flesh
hungrily have room, have space
to unloop its urgent arabesques.

Let your body leap and fly, wash
and flicker in the milk-foam light,
until there will be but one thing,
a white love moving.

And let the watching god be nameless
and beyond jealousy, because you do not know
from where this grace comes.

Marie, Marie, dance and dance. Give yourself
away. There is no more holding back.

The tomb effigies, broken-nosed, hands frozen
and folded in unlikely prayer, float and gleam
like drowned swimmers in milky surf

                    and high
in the black vault a lone bat, clinging
upside-down, senses you with his sonar,
and his small red eyes quiver as if in joy.

Lourdes, France

For My Father and Mother

Like great arks the long buses unload
the world's faces, the pinched eyes
and long jowls of the Slavs, the great
hooked nose of the Italians, the ruddy cheeks
and broken veins of the Germans, the paunches
and confidence of the Americans. These are
the middle-aged old, the halt, and the lame.

The young are not here. They are running
with the bulls in Pamplona, dancing *sur le pont
d'Avignon,* singing in Munich beer halls.

Here are only those who have held back,
who have never let go, who do not know
why life has passed them by without joy.
They come to ask the sober Lady for love.
To touch their flesh.

The youth are elsewhere kissing,
celebrating the great woman they cannot name
who courses in their veins like grass fire
crackling winter refuse above new sprouts.

O ma mere et mon pere, aging and gray
in a Kansas rest home, praying the rosary,

I pray, too, that you were once caught up
in that joy, assumed above the world,
in the crackling of stars, when perhaps if I
was lucky in the moment of my own conception,
my father hot from the hay and fresh
from the bullbarn, bulked above you
like a beyond-control god
and you were swept up in a grace
you would never have guessed,
and the galaxies opened and contracted
in quick flexings until you shouted
at the unexpected and surprising beauty.

How else could you have found
the calm to let your children grow
straight and tough as taproots

in a world where nearly everyone
has some limb so pitifully turned.
Nothing bent you, bone-deep, but love.

Here the twisted and the crippled go by.
They seem like you, good to the marrow,
but they are afraid of my eyes
and my notebook. They wonder what I am doing,
and they are not deeply sure about themselves.
Still they come and they come,
lame and contorted, gentle and kind.

The Woman Who Danced for the Devil

When I was only six I began
to dance for him, not because
I knew anything about sex
or Satan, but because only he
paid attention, could relish
what everyone else called bad.
Nakedness, forbidden, was a delight
that itched. Behind locked doors
I wrapped mine in colored scarves,
loose silk tingling my thin chest
and buttocks. Between bed and mirror,
I turned awkwardly, touching myself
into an electric glow, sensing
my father's head deliciously close
through the wall—I could hear
his newspaper ruffling. My small hips,
noiseless, moved in ways I had not
seen and did not have to learn.
Pushing my fingers at the folds
between my legs, I heard
music like the raw agitations
of great flocks of starlings, but rising
and clearing to the gold and green ice
of jarred chandeliers. Fire
small and cool, like first
flickerings under pyramided kindling,
my dance was less an invitation
than an offering, of small limbs, child

knees, to some bright exhilaration,
some adult-disdained, faraway
conflagration, but felt already
like the strike of sun on copper.

My need was simple as a sapling; I knew
nothing about trees. In my mother's shadow,
I hunted heat. In a landscape of frost,
only the devil had matches. It wasn't evil
I wanted, but incandescence, the sulfur
burn of my own presence.

Years later such dancing lured
grander gods and led to wild straddling
rides on the phallic broomstick, my hair
flinging back and forth like the loose hand
of a bull rider, lost and gone,
taken by moon flight, striking witch-terror
in any man less than Pan beneath me.
I found how long and deep I could
carry a cave of embers in shuddering
green dives through water-swirled light,
gliding down to black coral and fish-phosphor
in the prolonged luminescence
of his slow thrusting from behind.

It wasn't the devil, but was it
the child's daring that led me
in time to see and to love
how everything is deeply
on fire, heaped coals
ready to dance into flame.

Now in the shade of my tropic,
my children ripen like mangoes.

On ground cleared by crownfires,
I offer my hand, cool,
for the fevered head
of the unburned lost.

Wild Plum

Between Chateux Thierry and Epernay, we turn
the Volkswagen van into the Champagne hills,
away from the Marne up winding back roads,
past cultivated sunflower,
burnished July wheat, and the green
corrugations of hillside vineyards.

Sunlight rinses and sharpens edges,
is rubbed silver on weathered fenceposts,
on each wheat stem a gloss crystal.
Under the dark vines are fisted already
pale clusters of young grapes,
hard as marbles, that will ripen
clear and ferment so full of light
drinkers will think they are drinking stars.

Almost before we see it,
we have sped past a wild plum
glorious with fruit, spilling
heavy purple onto the narrow macadam.
By the time we wake to appetite
and chance, it is too late:
we are far down the steep road
and can only look back
at low branches and fallen fruit.

We ride on in clean light,
sorrowing, past the parallel purities

of young vines, feeling all the regret
of a missed sin. Fields of sunflowers
blaze yellow, acres of coronas
echoing the sun. But you and I hunger now
for purple excesses. Those plums hung
bright and bursting, a contrast
to this early summer promise, this
tight rounded perfection of new grapes
and pubescent girls before they swell
heavy into hot and wakened womanhood.

Those plums were swollen and soft
like your sundark nipple
I first saw on the Riviera beach.
They were the purple of kings,
tumescent, like the swelling mouth
of an insatiable woman.

Suddenly as if longing conjured it,
another plum tree ahead!
I swerve off under low branches.
You scramble atop the van to reach,
legs spread so your feet perch
on the luggage rack corners. Your short
denim skirt stretches pale blue
across tan thighs, the soft fruit
showering down from jarred branches,
a hail of purple
pummeling my head and shoulders.
I bite and suck a plum, the juice
flowing down my beard.

Above me laughing open-mouthed, suddenly rich
and free among the hills, you gather
and cradle plums in the lifted tuck
of your blouse. Around us now France ripens
into summer; everywhere in field and fence row
the Great Mother moves in severe light
and shadow humming her melody of fruit.
And you, her tan-thighed daughter, robed in pale blue
on an orange van above grapegreen wheatgold hills
spill purple plums and promise from full hands
and blouse.

Singing of Black

All these years I have lived in bright rooms,
the night has leaned against the locked windows
like a lonely woman, and I have not seen her!
The windows squaring the dark
gave me back
my small self
in the lamp's light.

Now I stand in the door
framed by light
and feel the dark's dark eyes
her long fingers softly learning
the curve of my shoulder, the slant of my thigh.

Lithe daughter, Isis child,
because you have given yourself
to me, the night is full: I open
my arms and my mouth to the darkness, my lungs
heave with the night's breathing.

Now the night and I love each other!
She refuses to leave me, even in the day—
she hangs on in the dark sheathes of my shoes,
in the whorl of the shell from the sea,
in the cup of my own hand!
Yes, now, naked and lovely, and singing of black,
she bathes all day in the well of my ear.

What Mel, Drinking, Writes
After the Beautiful Woman Departs

You are a lake at sunset where a single teal flashes
    green and blue wings away toward grey distance.
You are the flutter of the robin in the rainwater pooled
    on the lawn,
the first step on land after a long day in a canoe,
the regathering of quail in the long grass,
the huddling down of the blue-throated barnswallow
    in her rafter-hung nest.

You are the softness on the mossy horns of the giraffe,
the bounce of the ball landing over the fence in the
    last half of the tenth,
fresh bread set golden and tender on the oventop,
the laughter of a daring woman at the edge of the
    streetlight's reach.

You are the sweet whorl in the water the beaver leaves
    when she launches from shore,
the fresh bandage wrapped with long gentle fingers,
the dream-smile of the sleeping newborn.

You are a child racing with Easter-basket toward a clump
    of lilies,
the long stretch on the bed after a day of hard labor,
the dewdrop on the iris's beard at sunup,
the spill of quarters in the slot-machine tray.

You are the sweated curl on the neck of a dark-haired
    woman dancing the cha-cha-cha.
the heart curve of her hips belted small at the waist,
the distant train whistle through falling snow,
the sesame seed on the glazed roll passed back to the
    rumble seat of a blue roadster.

You are the smell of fresh linen in a swept room where
    a jonquil and a candle burn.

VI.

HOME GROUND

Tara Hill

I have slept where the kings have slept
high on the hill
at Tara

I.

Through sheep and wind I walk up Tara hill
and gaze at the land till my breath grows still.
For miles the rolling ground falls green away
in the hummocked pastures of the High Kings' day.
Only the curve of the earth horizoned the King
where land and sky meet in a distant ring.
Tara's kings were cattle kings, and could be still,
for today only wind and cattle keep Tara's hill:
the kings are gone, the halls all down,
not a harp is left, not a minstrel's sound.
The once-proud stronghold ring-forts slump
in shallow circles where the burials hump.
In prodigious earth works greatly worn,
all that sparkles is the nettle's thorn,
and the feet of persistent rain that centuries sweep
like drifts of cattle through the ancient keep.

I lay down on that windwalked ground
and dreamed a dream my heart has kept,
and a line that sings *for I have slept*
where the kings have slept
high on the hill
at Tara.

II.

The kings were strong, so legends claim,
and poets believed, before the Christians came.
Then all that seemed immortal was Tara's grace.
The chiefs were gathered for the annual Feis,
Laoghaire ready to light the Samhan flame,
when Patrick's fire flared first on the Hill of Slane
and burned like anger in the pagan eyes
of Dadaanan Celts watching from the Tara skies.
But Tara's fall was general, the cause far worse
than Brendan's anger or Ruadhan's curse.
Those bishops too from the hill have gone
and everything they placed their cross upon.
In the valley churchyard where lizards crawl
Christian weeds and eroded gravestones sprawl.
There amid jackdaw cry and raven "craw"
Patrick's church stands stuffed with straw.

Oh, all shall sleep as the kings have slept
high on the hill
at Tara

III.

Over Ireland grey sea-storms daily blow
and shake the heart with what the mind can know.
I have heard what wind with a wet mouth can say
through Kerry mist and fog at the close of day.
I have seen boulders strewn in the Dingle rain
like skulls of years that time has slain.
I have watched a razor tongue flicker and play
in black clouds flung down on Bantry Bay.
The sun was sharp one moment on Knocknarea,

but the bones in the barrow could not see.
There were no eyes for the light to find.
The stones of the mound, and Maeve, are blind.
Yeats' name on the tavern and his stone is graved
(beer and tourists praise him whom beauty slaved).
But Yeats lies low in his Drumcliff bed
while Sligo rain beats down Ben Bulben's head.

They, too, sleep as the kings have slept
high on the hill
at Tara.

IV.
Everything obeys the general decree:
the Cliffs of Moher dive to the sea.
The golden gorse, the foxgloves' purple glow—
all end in the black and white of death and snow.
Though from boulders in sun the birds insist,
I see the knuckled bones of the mountain's fist.
In every symphony I hear the rattling cart
playing the descant notes. Oh, sometimes in the heart
the brightest beach falls under a cloud
and death, drunk on wet and cold, gets loud.

For I must sleep as the kings have slept
high on the hill
at Tara.

V.
But life is sweet because death is tart:
brevity is beauty in roses and in the heart.
So I must live as the kings lived here

when the blood ran hot and life was dear,
where the wind blows unblocked and keen
and the summer light wears a peacock sheen.
Because of a dream on a windswept hill
I will say each day *I will; I will.*
I will celebrate, in rain, the rainbow weather;
answer, in fair, the soft invitations of heather.
Still there is a seed in the self that sings,
a glory that grows in the hatchling's wings.
Though the light lie down and the heather go,
I will live such love, it will burn the snow!

For I have slept where the kings sleep still
high on the hill
at Tara.

Gold Notes

Stepping into Easter
dawn, cool, bird-laced
dew-jeweled, light-sprung

returning home,
picking long-stemmed, a jonquil—
breakfast table surprise

(the jonquil is a horn
jazzing the spring
toward Easter)

Next day, spring's first neighbor
bringing us a fistful
smaller, paler

Today, quiet above them
in the same green vase,
ours is a tall gold eye

soft periscope
into all our corners

Christmas Ferns

(Polysticum Acrostichoides)

I walk out early Easter morning to see what my plants are up to. Up and down the avenue, the neighbors' lawns purr soft and green, lined up along the street flat as nursing kittens. In my front yard there is a snow of strawberries in bloom, and beneath the white blossoms, in the heavy shadow of leaves, slugs slide back to dark beds where the pine straw is already asleep hugging the earth, having decided to stay there forever. Along the edge of the yard blueberry branches are heavy with honeycombs of bloom, and rhubarb plants are making their first powerful thrust out of the earth like red fists . . . like babies' heads adorned with placental blood. Young dwarf apple trees whose branching scaffold of whips stood cut back to stubby candelabra all winter have flared at every tip with new green flames. The peach blossoms have fallen and all along the branches tiny fruit swells, still trailing long pistillate tails like sperm.

But what are these strange fantastic things here along the unused walk . . . where the fallen fronds of ferns dug from the woods last year have lain wet and torn in the pine litter all winter? There are bulging clusters of silver furry things exploding through the ground, crowding together like people bursting out of the doors of a coliseum! I kneel down to get a closer look. Most of them are curled tight as eggs against the earth, but others have pushed up and begun to unfurl, unrolling like paper New-Years-party favors. A few have rolled all the way up and open, into miniature waving fronds, delicate green and silver.

The way these things spin upward, they could be a volley of skyrockets being sent up by the slow ant people for some insect 4th of July. The ones that have whirled up just half way stand curled like shepherds' staves stuck in the ground . . . like the protruding scroll and neck of a bass viol whose music still pulses in the halls of the underworld. I move around to the other side on my hands and knees . . . the new sun haloes them now from behind . . . so that their hairs glisten and stand out like a shimmer of Kirlian light. No, now I see . . . these earliest standing fronds are furred and feathered like delicate antennae, . . . and these slower stronger ones coming up below are the uncurling tongues of great butterflies that have been asleep under the earth!

Fenceposts

Last fall, making yet another thing
from materials at hand, and knowing
the penalties for such grace, I cut
small trees close to the clearing—
willow oak, tulip poplar, sweetgum,
whatever offered itself thigh-thick
and straight. Though steel posts would
last thirty years, and these rot
in three or four, these were here now, ready
for use, and free, and I liked their bark
and tang. I liked the ironwoods' ridged
and corded muscles popping my own
pectorals slick with sweat.

All winter in swirling wind from the woods
the posts stood frozen in a perfect row,
new wire gleaming like musical staves,
and here and there for moments carrying
a notation of blackbirds, and sometimes
a cardinal, like a drop of Mozart's blood.

Now in spring when I go with seeds to scratch
wounds in the fenced field, I'm astonished
to notice a post putting up leaves,
and then find one after another, most of them
stirring to life, foolish with sap, busting green
through rough bark, believing, believing.

Hey fellows, you're dead! I cut your throats.

Myths tell of kings who, thrusting a staff
into the ground to mark a sacred spot or say
Here I will build my city, returned to find
the staff blossoming, sapling for the central tree.

How many Camelots have I created here?

These lopped limbs are not oleander, raintree,
yggdrasil ash. They are commoners struck down
in their prime. Like so many of us, they will
start nothing, leave nothing behind. July heat
will wither them, tell them loud:
You shall not go on.

But in April who listens?
This morning even I may grow
deaf for a moment in the garden
watching seeds dive from my hand
into dirt where the dead are living.

Listening

Trying to relearn a folk habit,
we sit in the yard while night falls,
talking quietly, fingering the day's minor
notes. Our swing drifts back and forth
under the arbor. Unpressed, the talk
laves and flows, directionless.
Darkness begins to smoke
from the clustered grapes.

The dogs lie belly down on the lawn
near us, ears up, their gaze faraway—
in dream space. Then I remember.
That posture—the farm dogs listening
like that in Kansas forty years ago.
My parents sat under the cedars
at nightfall talking gardens and weather.
With the dogs, we lay on the grass
under the words dissolving
into susurrus, a rhythm of content.
Their voices were steady, changing
only as ripe wheat moves, ripples
and remains. Something in the sound
reaches across time, smoothes years
in seamless murmur and flow.

Was it this that brought the wolf in
from the wood? That all the animals
circled close to hear in Orpheus' voice?

How many centuries of nights
did the wolf lie golden-eyed listening
in the fringe of trees, longing
to creep closer, to lie near the circle
of light, letting men's words range in his ears
like his own easy loping in the hills,
changing directions, going somewhere
undetermined, following a scent
or an intuition, veering
forward, one with the terrain.

Is this what these dogs so love to be near,
what I so loved as a child and remember tonight
like a wolf learning to lie by the low fire
of our voices, like a man learning
to turn his words loose in the dark.

Dreaming and Waking Beside the River Aare

(near Berne, Switzerland)

Driving all day half-blinded by Bavaria in bloom,
I fall all night down the steep stairs of sleep,
and just before morning I dream the celestial city,
walk the New Jerusalem; joy and the bladed sun
strong on the white buildings, the mica
chirruping from the flagstones, horses
shimmering thighs in the long grass, trees lifted
and singing in vertical chorus,
and all my senses rinsed,
and perfect, and at home

—and waking in the warm sheets,
my body glowing beside yours, I lift up
and look outside the van window
at the surprise of a world in fresh light,
the world I have dreamed! It is all here,
lying open and real, green and blooming
beneath the snow mountains,
beside the ice-cold emerald Aare.

Bavarian Housebarns

Bavarians have it all together:
house and barn, bulls and babies;
manure pile ripening sweet
beneath the kitchen window
where pies are set to cool;
silage trenched and covered
next to the wall; zinnias wide
as dinnerplates in the dooryard,
tulips big as beersteins;
and each morning the Brown Swiss
leaving downstairs, passing the study window
on their way back to the long grass.

I try to imagine what it would be like
living in a house with animals
in the lap of the Alps and the almighty:
on cold evenings, churning the butter
before low hearthfire, while the cows
lie heavily in the basement below, chewing
their cuds with half-closed eyes; the butter
beginning to come in the churn, rich
nuggets like islands in the swimming cream,
like stars in the great Milky Way above us;
and late at night lying beside my lover, hearing
beneath my bed, the stanchioned bull, aroused,
against the wood of his manger,
hooking, hooking, hooking.

Like Any Animal

Hungry and sure like any animal,
I love you slowly,
fearlessly in the open grass.
Your flesh is like black water.
Rapids shimmer the cottonwood.
Moon froth spills a lace of surf
over the hillside. The watching
fox rests his head on his paws.

We could be anywhere or nowhere,
tide winds rocking the sea oats,
white sands humped and duned,

your pleasure diving again
and again beneath the waves
until the moon herself
slides into the water

and I too drown at last
and float, headless,
given, out to sea.

Lolled on our backs,
above us the stars
as they always have been,
lights on in the house,
and we, at home.

The Gift

In this unlooked for,
unasked for moment,
sitting at the kitchen table
looking into the next room,
I all at once see
what has been there
how long?

Sunlight fills the room corner
in a geometry of shadow and brilliance,
lifts the picture molding,
the shining hinges of a door,
the white mopboard;
and in my own simple house,
empty of everything,
I am Vermeer and Van Eyck
and the spirit lives in white paint
and light and blue wall
and through the angle
of a yet farther door and farther room
and window, a still
different blue sky,

and in the middle ground
a fish bowl, collecting light
like a dragon in bliss,
reflects lintel and post
and blinds, and a red bow

from the child's hair
discarded on the white table.
Light like a blade on the wall,
in the fishless water and bowl
bounced, and arced, and repeated.

I look down to write this,
and look up, and am amazed.
In one moment the light has gone,
and except for my eyes,
and these words,
never was.

A Room of Our Own

After making love, they lie quietly.
She thinks out loud. "It would be good
for us. I mean, this is a nice room,
but we should have one of our own,
one nobody knows about, a secret room.
It wouldn't need to be anywhere,
you know . . . just inside us. Okay?

We'd have to furnish it, though, I guess.
Wouldn't we? I know it would have icicles
hanging inside close to the window, so we can
break and suck them when we are hot from loving.
Sometimes the sun hitting them throws
rainbows on the bed." She pauses, thinking.
"The bed is in the middle of the room," she says.

"It's a round bed," he says. "Big enough so
our loving can pivot, like the hands of a clock
around the center. And it has flowers growing
from the middle. Whenever you pick one, another
reappears in its place. You like the iris best."

"Is there any other furniture?" she asks.
Then answers herself: "There should be vines,
I think. Vines. All over the walls and ceiling.
But the room had to have other furniture at first,
didn't it? You know, ordinary, familiar furniture,
or at least at first I would have been afraid

to go into it with you. Not now, I wouldn't,
I wouldn't be afraid now, because you are known
to me, all over, even under my fingernails.

"Maybe now," he says, "the room has a tree stump,
still resinous and smelling of cedar.
Where the rings are tiniest, there's a small cleft
where you stick feathers you find in the woods."

"And books," she says, "lots of books."

"Yes," he says, "and music. And the moon.
Remember how the moon checked on us that first night
from the skylight, and then looked in again
as it fell past the naked trees
in the west windows at dawn."

"Yes," she says, "Nobody else
has a room and a moon like that."

"Nobody," he says.

Stalled

A whole hour for once I have
stalled empty almost
in a trance the world
of work dissolved nothing
happening inside nor outside
the dogs stretched under the cool
of the gardenhouse the cat sprawled
in the ferns the surrounding green
the pecan the high mulberry the wild
hedgerow something here feels
loved quietly and for sure
in the mimosa an inner eyelid
slides over the thrasher's eye
the body likes this
and remembers itself
ten thousand years mute

Home Ground

Where I pumped water for them
at the well-curb, a crowd of cedar waxwings
pretend their serious arguments.
In the winter tulip bed a squirrel
peels the husk from a black walnut,
turning it in his hands like a lathe.
Another finishes last night's leftover
cornbread high in the hackberry.
A chicadee and a purple finch
wait for the cardinal
to finish at the feeder.
Breakfast coffee idles in my hand
at the window. I am home again.
In the deep well, the water drops,
falling back into themselves,
are singing.

Acknowledgments

These poems have previously appeared as indicated:
"Chilton County Woods" in *Southern Poetry Review*; "Dachau"
and "Facing the Light" in *Octoberfest*; "Fenceposts" and "How
My Father Milked" in *Southern Humanities Review*; "The Gift"
in *Sunflower Petals*; "Gold Notes," "Mel Prunes His Flowers,"
and "Stocking the Pond" in *Aura*; "Letting the Garden Go,"
"Listening," "Lourdes, France," and "Six Portraits of Magdalene"
in *Birmingham Poetry Review*; "Leaving Home" and "Singing of
Black" in *Contemporary Literature in Birmingham*; "Leaving
Home," "Singing of Black," and "Variations on a Zen Apho-
rism," in *Alabama Poets*; "Lighting the Lamp" and "Watching
My Mother's Breath" in *Beloit Poetry Journal*; "Love Song" and
"Singing of Black" in *Thunder City Broadsides*; "Mockingbird"
in *The Midwest Quarterly*; "Moving the Snake" in *Red Mountain
Rendezvous*; "Wild Plum" in *Astarte*; and "Singing of Black,"
"Gold Notes," and "Christmas Ferns" in *The Isis Poems*.

About the Author

JIM MERSMANN now lives on a small Alabama farm following Walt Whitman's longing to "turn and live with the animals." Before retiring from the English Department at the University of Alabama at Birmingham, he won numerous teaching and writing awards including the Birmingham Chamber of Commerce's Silver Bowl for Literature, the Ellen Gregg Ingalls Award for Excellence in Classroom Teaching, and the UAB Honors Program Outstanding Faculty Award, as well as a Fulbright Professorship to teach in Rio de Janeiro. His poems have appeared as *The Isis Poems* and in *The Southern Poetry Review, The Southern Humanities Review, The Beloit Poetry Journal, The Midwest Quarterly, The Birmingham Poetry Review,* and other journals. His literary criticism includes articles on contemporary poets, a monograph on Allen Ginsberg, and *Out of the Vietnam Vortex: A Study of Poets and Poetry Against the War.*

www.ingramcontent.com/pod-product-compliance
Lightning Source LLC
Chambersburg PA
CBHW022025090426
42739CB00006BA/287